YOU'RE GONNA LOVE THIS

YOU'RE GONNA LOVE THIS

POEMS
BY

DINA DEL BUCCHIA

TALONBOOKS

Talonbooks
9259 Shaughnessy Street, Vancouver, British Columbia, Canada V6P 6R4
talonbooks.com

Talonbooks is located on xʷməθkʷəy̓əm, Sḵwx̱wú7mesh, and səlilwətaɬ Lands.

First printing: 2024

Typeset in Arno
Printed and bound in Canada on 100% post-consumer recycled paper

Cover image: *Woman On Television*, CSA Images

Talonbooks acknowledges the financial support of the Canada Council for the Arts, the Government of Canada through the Canada Book Fund, and the Province of British Columbia through the British Columbia Arts Council and the Book Publishing Tax Credit.

Library and Archives Canada Cataloguing in Publication

Title: You're gonna love this : poems / by Dina Del Bucchia.
Other titles: You are gonna love this
Names: Del Bucchia, Dina, 1979- author.
Identifiers: Canadiana 20230557562 | ISBN 9781772016123 (softcover)
Subjects: LCGFT: Poetry.
Classification: LCC PS8607.E482538 Y68 2024 | DDC C811/.6—dc23

For Jason

Television! Teacher, mother, secret lover.
—HOMER SIMPSON
"Treehouse of Horror V," *The Simpsons* (1994)

You wake me up when I fall
asleep [1] on the remote. Nudge me,

tell me exactly what I'm doing.
"You fell asleep watching TV."

I complain, don't want to be
disturbed. I'm busy absorbing

stories in my sleep. Osmosis,
something ephemeral enters

the brain. But you stay
pragmatic, don't give up, pull

me upright, so I
can stumble to bed, dream

of the things I've seen. In life
and onscreen.

1.   This happens way too much.

The woman who hosted *Romper Room* [2]
never once said my name. I'm not the only one.
I liked Mr. Do-Bee, [3] and the songs,
but deep down I just wanted
that fucking woman to say
she saw me in her mirror-less mirror!
But then I'd get to the end
and feel empty again. Maybe
the first time a reality
disappointed. I wanted a famous person
to acknowledge me in the most important
box I knew: the television.

2. Please get in touch if you too want to complain about this *Romper Room* erasure of your name.

3. The concept of the Do-Bee is kind of problematic. Like, not if you're thinking about improv, but it's okay to say "don't" and "no." It took me forty years to get there, but eventually I got there. This bee was propaganda for Big Parent to get kids to behave! This bee wanted us to "yes, and ..." through life.

I fought sleep so much as a kid,
never wanted to go to bed, had FOMO before FOMO
was an abbrev. I stayed up for adult sitcoms, the only
eight-year-old who wanted to recap *Moonlighting*
on the playground the next day. *Cheers, Night Court*, anything
with adults cracking wise. Now that I'm an adult,
I know I'm a Diane Chambers. I've got a master's degree.
I work in the service industry. I would eat
Sam Malone for breakfast.

I wasn't some indoor kid. I grew up literally
at the base of a mountain forest. I fell out
of trees building forts, nails swiped from coffee
cans in the shed, boards nicked from an old fence.
I swam in lakes, rivers, creeks, swimmin' holes.
I worried about leeches, wasps, ticks.
I played street hockey, built snow forts,
rode a GT Sno Racer through a trail we tamped down
with our own boots.

I ask if you want to finish *Game of Thrones*,
and you shrug. And I support that. But I've

started this ride, and I need to stay on the roller coaster
until the dragons die, the incest crushed in rubble.

When I start something I know would appeal,
I try again, but you tell me you're not interested.

You're Gen X, but mimic Gen Z, watch YouTube,
visual podcasts about wrestling. I see you perk

up when they mention your favourites,
current, or from your youth, deep WWF/E.

You seem to have given up on television
but I'm just getting started. I'm deep in.

It's not cable, it's illegal downloads, a found
friend that keeps me from deep thoughts

related to myself, to the ways your body
is rejecting activities you used to enjoy.

I make a list of all the ones I want to rewatch,
revisit, as if that brings back a past time,

better moments for our bodies, our weepy
brains. *Enlightened* and *Carnivàle* are comfort,

despite the anxiety, the stress, the grotesque
ways humans interact when they want to be better

when the lines between good and evil are drawn
in the dust-bowl sand or semi-permanent Sharpie

on a white board. When Laura Dern screams
in the bathroom stall, mascara streaming

in that shot of her in the pilot, I feel it.
I want to scream, sometimes I do scream,

but I am quiet, watching, yearning for a valid
reason to scream my frustration. Instead

I stay in bed and watch three more episodes
in silence. I hold in my pee because the covers

are warm and smell of too many days without
a wash. You're in here too, a subtle scent.

She wants the world to be a better place, but
no one has articulated the term "white feminism"

to her or about her. Taking down one corporation
still leaves the foundational corporate structure. Amid

her self-help leanings, her new-age heart, there is pure
inclination to help, and a stubborn drive to connect.

A show to come back to, relevant in how we try
to function as a society. Underground tech bunkers

filled with people being underpaid, a woman living
with her mother because she broke down, lost it.

Shit. Am I Hannah from *Girls*?[4]

4.   I mean, am I lacking self-awareness while pretending I have total self-awareness, but the awareness is so narrow it's like barely being aware at all?

TGIF was not really TGIF to me. Despite
the entire premise being
a celebratory ending to the week
in front of the television.
It stressed me out to hear the jokes
delivered with such intense purpose.
I was supposed to care about catchphrases and why
DJ was being such a bitch that day.
Try to figure out how to get my bangs
to look like Kimmy Gibbler's. I couldn't
care. What's popular with kids isn't
always bad, but what's marketed to them
can be. I didn't learn anything from
watching Urkel pull his pants up inside
himself, but I learned about myself,
I was ready to go it alone, without
the coziness of cultural company.

Even though years later I'd turn to teen programming,
the cloying appeal of friendships that never end,
I couldn't give myself over to raunchy comedians
as dads. Pop culture clicked when I learned
Alanis had gone down on Dave "Cut It Out"
Coulier in a theatre. That John Stamos got
hotter as he aged. That mullets were a moment
we were lucky to live through.

And I hadn't even read any critical works
yet, was unaware of the concept of criticism.
Then, I wasn't able to connect to kids
about what I watched on TV. Their
parents weren't letting them stay up
to watch adult sitcoms, didn't set
the VCR for SNL.

Being a snob as a kid is so humiliating.

I don't want to do what people tell me to do. Even a TV show recommendation I take reluctantly. I think it's a common feeling for people who are stubborn or tired or have strong ideas of self. Maybe stubborn and strong ideas of self are the same thing but I'm trying to dress it up. Westerns are usually terrible to me, but somehow one was recommended to me, won me over, and I had to admit it was great. I have ridden horses and it's overrated. Have other people felt like they didn't enjoy genre stories until one turned them around? It's a good feeling I wish I felt more often. There's some kind of pretentious veneer I'm scared to crack. [5] And every time I try to tell friends to watch this show, the skepticism on their faces is so intense I start to think I might be wrong. But I love it so. I love that show. I fucking can't not love it.

5.   This is absolutely despite having truly terrible taste in many other ways, including how much I love trash snacks, will defend refined sugar as a way of life, and that I watched so many episodes of *Toddlers & Tiaras*, *Say Yes to the Dress*, *Trading Spaces*, *Blind Date*, and *What Not to Wear* in my twenties.

We started *Deadwood* skeptical. A show full of villains
and outsiders because that's what the old west was.

They made their own rules and forced
Indigenous people out. We would climb

into bed with my laptop, the first of many
MacBooks I'd purchase despite

always having to buy a new MacBook. You could
call him Al[6] because it was his name. You

could call out, "Cocksucker," because why not?
The sheriff has an anger management issue

and I was always hitting my forehead in frustration
because I couldn't get you to react to my emotions

even in a high-intensity disagreement. Balled fists
making contact with my temples, flat palms

reddening skin above my eyebrows. I was not mellow,
you could be chill to my outbursts.

We were different. Except we both
wanted other people to do what we said,

what we told them to do, but that's not
what people do. Even if you love them.

Even if you are there for them, even if you
take care of them.

6.   With apologies to Paul Simon, but never Chevy Chase.

I watched *Survivor* season 1
during my second summer with you.

I worked shift work at an industrial plant,
in 2000, and still it's the most I've ever made

at an hourly wage, over twenty years later. Life is like
an immunity challenge. You never know

if you're going to make $24 an hour again.
But probably not. Everyone loses. No alliance.

I fell asleep in the bar on *Survivor* night.[7]
Server tried to kick me out, but you stopped

them, said, "She's not drunk, just between
day and night shift. Can we get some onion rings?"

7.   Why only watch sports in a bar? Why are there only sports bars and not awards
      show bars, or reality TV bars? I suppose heteronormativity is at play, but sports
      are pretty queer. It feels like no one wants to talk about either of these things.
      If people want to do Jägerbombs and watch the series finale of *This Is Us*, then
      more power to them.

I broke up with *America's Next Top Model*
after cycle twenty. Which is a long run. One day
I changed the channel at the regular time
and I couldn't look at these young
wannabe models, couldn't imagine
watching more hours of them
put through social experiments[8] as farce.
I just couldn't. I'm not sorry. And with it,
every other reality competition toppled.
I've never watched an entire episode
of *Drag Race*. Can you believe it? I can't
handle these soothing baking shows[9] everyone
tries to sell me on. I prefer eating
baked goods. Watching the trifle get made
doesn't do anything for me. It's certainly
not doing a thing for my tastebuds or brain.
My favourite way to get high.

8. Experiments include: walking a twelve-inch runway in a giant hamster ball on water, photoshoots in blackface, Tyra pretending to faint in front of the models to scare them, walking a runway with swinging pendulums, a treadmill runway, a vertical runway, and walking a runway with THEIR HANDS SET ON FIRE.
9. *Nailed It!* is not included in this because it's chaos, and Nicole Byer is the most charming and hilarious host, and her TV friendship with Jacques Torres is pure delight.

HGTV infuriates me. [10] People buying homes
is the least relatable kind of content. Maybe
this is why it's popular. Or maybe I'm wrong,
and people watch it because they own property
with buildings on that property, dwellings. Even sheds.
I'm not sure how something so tedious
became entertainment. It's like procedurals.
I'm too much and they all bore me and enrage me
in equal measure. Make something interesting happen!
Do not show me another identical second bedroom.
Please, I am begging you. There are people
with actual ideas who could make television shows
for you instead. But I understand. These are cheap
in production cost and quality. Corporations clearly
can't afford anything worthwhile.

10.   But I would watch a show just about bidets and Japanese toilets.

Did reality TV become meaningless to me because I became one of those assholes who said, "I have real problems; who gives a fuck about the Kardashians? They can't take away my pain!" Maybe. More likely something clicked in me and the manufactured reality stopped working. It no longer had any power over my head and heart. There's so much of it. It's unfortunate I can't imbibe something so plentiful, have it fulfill my needs. It's like when a medication stops working for you and you realize you can't take it anymore. A painkiller that can't kill pain, a pill that won't relieve a headache. An entire genre stopped doing its homeopathic job.

When we were roommates, Roxan and I
watched *American Idol* and rooted

for Kelly Clarkson from the beginning. Good for her!
We spent so much time drinking cheap drinks,

smoking out the second-storey window, watching basic
cable after class. You and Rox would taunt me by loving

Judging Amy, which I refused to indulge in, mostly because
I always fell asleep when it was on. Mocking me

while I drooled on the second-hand sofa. TLC
was an important part of our dinners when we

cooked together. *Trading Spaces* made us think
about how we could try to make our two-bedroom

rental more us, and less undergraduates with no money.
Even though undergraduates with no money was who we

were. We painted the bathroom red. And unplugged
the phone for most of six months when we all

got behind on our bills. Kept cable. Kept up with
what we were not supposed to wear.

My original watch of *Carnivàle* was after wisdom-
tooth surgery. The needles hurt and I cried.

From the waiting room you heard my wails.
Back then, you weren't too sick to come with me,

to make sure I had what I needed. I didn't have to be
in pain alone. I was cared for at that time.

I sat in the dark for days watching "freaks"
and believers move through a mythology

that felt real, even though critics said
it was too convoluted. It made sense to me.

Puzzles to solve, tarot, and Ferris wheels.
I could only have water, T3s, PC-brand ice cream.

The second time I watched *Carnivàle*,
years later, it was after we'd been renovicted

and were spending hundreds more dollars
a month to live a few blocks away. Characters

hovering in a dark light, jewel and earth tones
that made me feel safe as I watched people

cope with strange dangers at every turn.
There's magic in this show, even though

so many people suffer, keep dying, try
to live amid demons and unknowns. I'm jealous

of their camaraderie, together in a caravan
every moment. You've been out for coffee for hours.

Your attempt to wake up, feel alert. I click the Apple
remote, plug another episode into my brain. Clea DuVall,

beautiful, pouts righteously in the dust bowl, her slacks
billowing, she exhales smoke, more turmoil in the air.

I can sense you smoking in the alley, invisible to me,
but I know, though our bedroom is a windowless box.

I stay on lockdown in bed. Bladder ready to burst. Until
you unlock the door. Sigh as you enter.

I close my laptop as a fire starts in the carnival.
Don't say hello to you, cover my head, and hope I fall asleep.

I can't watch any more crime dramas
and yet somehow a computer thinks it's all I need
and unlike me the algorithm doesn't mind being wrong,
it persists, it pushes me. "Try this! What about this?
You like this, so you will definitely fall in love with this
and more!" I just want something that brings
genuine human feeling and also numbs
the parts of me I am not in the mood for.
Is that too much to ask? Netflix thinks so.

I'm wrong for wanting so much
distraction. I'm wrong for relying
on constant entertainment. But I am still watching
after three episodes even though I fell asleep
two episodes ago because I didn't even
like what I was watching. Not that we always
have to like what we're watching. We're trained
to be around people we dislike all the time.
That's work, every day, go in, make money,
work enough hours to retain benefits.

I knew things were starting to get weird when I didn't care who did the murdering. Everything felt familiar, boring instead of comfortable and pleasing. I would rather watch rumpled British people do anything besides solve a crime. Go to clown college, build a birdhouse, yell at each other in a pub over darts. Is it a betrayal of my middle-aged ladydom to not want to exclusively watch tedious crime shows, with their low light and horribly ugly and practical waterproof jackets? I see that every day in Vancouver. And I'm sure some intense, high-tech, shorts-clad cyclists have killed. We have more militarized police here now with all sorts of tools and they still can't catch murderers.

Respecting authority is one of the worst traits a person can have.

Chronic illness isn't easy. Not like placid
cooking shows that make it look effortless to create

a perfect meal. It's work. Every day,
a loving slog to get to a place of hope for you.

On TV people get better or they die. You
are in limbo. Very *Twin Peaks* of you,

I've never been diagnosed anything. Am I
allowed to even allude to being depressed?

Permitted to feel bad? Or is that only for
people on antidepressants? I avoid diagnoses

because I'm supposed to be fun, the extrovert,
a classic Leo. Loyal, drop anything to help.

But when I look back, I've only got
this cable subscription

for a few more weeks, and that renoviction notice
but no one to accurately tell me the difference

between an anxiety attack and a panic attack
except the internet who, let's face it, can't even

make the distinction between actual nazis and people
asking for the nazis to be banned from nazi-ing

online and my doctor who barely says a word to me
no matter how distressed I look. He doesn't engage

in communication, stares at me while I try my best
to explain why I feel like my body and brain

have conspired against me by deciding to never
work together anymore. I miss my old doctor,

a real character. She would gently slap my leg after
every pelvic exam, always told me I did a great job,

when all I had to do was scooch forward and lie
there with my crotch in her face for a few minutes.

TV doctors are either dramatic or bumbling.
I will not be moved on this point, this stereotype.

I never much got into shows about hospitals,
a smattering here and there. A splattering of blood

for comedic effect in a dark comedy, that way
I knew mortality was in the mix, but I didn't

have to confront long, drawn-out romantic scenes.
Why are TV hospitals [11] so ripe for boning down?

The classic proximity of sex and death.
It's a little obvious don't you think? Procedurals

make me feel so little hope for humanity.

---

11. Hospitals on television are based on sex and death. The most basic of human
     functions. It's strange that no one has truly been able to create realism in a
     hospital drama. Where are the fluorescent lights that give out headaches for
     free with every trip to the ER?

Olivia Pope takes coats seriously, I love her for it.
Her coats safely closet-kept when she prepares
dinner, table set near her pristine
white couch. A tray with two courses:
popcorn poured into a bowl,
red wine poured into a bowl-sized glass. Perfect posture,
loungewear goals as she sits in cashmere sweats,
the kind that are too nice for me to know
about. I would swirl right onto a cushion,
break trust with the delicate roughness
of the ways of Olivia Pope. She brings
goldfish bowl–sized wineglass to her lips
and inhales, breathes deep the tannins, the hints
not like the ones she tapes up at work, clues
adorning the windows of an office space,
so unassuming. No, at home, she is not like me,
she slinks into silence, a nest for resting thoughts.
Everything minimalist and somehow lush.
But sometimes, even there she's interrupted.
Men do not give her a moment's peace. They
have keys for all her locks, cameras in nooks,
eyes that watch, hands that grab. The dream
of being a powerful woman, competent,
aggressive, beautiful, and deserving of care.
She's busted up again and again. I watch for
these commercial-interrupted escapes
where Olivia Pope can't even enjoy a goddamn
glass of wine. Because though she tries,
her home is a disruption, a barrier to chill.
How much are we alike,
Olivia Pope? I would say a small amount, but
my home is not my sanctuary and when people say
trite things like that I feel ready to turn on them
with a Papa Pope–level monologue.

Winter is long. Rainy. Cold. I work sixty hours a week and it's still barely enough to have a life. I bundle myself in blankets, another layer over my fleece otter onesie and cardigan. I watch the sky, a dog pissing on the tiny spots of weeds down the alley. It would be a dream to walk around more often without an umbrella, but a bigger dream would be to live in some kind of alternate reality. Where I could control the weather. Maybe I do like superhero stories after all. I like a fantasy, but prefer it's not capital *F*. The fantasy of having a more interesting life. The fantasy of blowing up my own life. The fantasy of never having to do domestic chores. Usually, they don't show that on television unless they want to punish a character, or they did a murder [12] and have to clean it up, or it's a simplistic and reductive way to show a character is in mental distress, or they're avoiding something else. Scrubbing a toilet is a narrative tool.

12. I think a murderer would be great to hire as a cleaner. But they probably need motivation to get out the stains.

We are in the ER again and you don't want to cry
but do want to cry and I am here and not chain-smoking

at the Odyssey, which is what I'm thinking about. Menthol drags
and whatever cocktail is on special that night. You're the one

slumped over, then going outside to the sidewalk to hack butts,
while I wait inside in case they call your name.

Shows about doctors bore me. I've spent enough time
in the ER with you. Waiting to get relief that never comes.

At first, they tell you it's sciatica, nothing more,
which isn't saying sciatica is nothing, it's not.

Getting a doctor is harder than getting affordable housing.
You come home again, months later,

defeated. Clear your own doc doesn't want to deal
with anything related to illness that can't be

easily fixed, that might require long-term
management, and care. Next appointment

I'm in the office too, getting heated, questioning
his authority, because it's shitty, and he's shitty. [13]

I can't tell if you're embarrassed or grateful
as we quietly ride the bus home.

13.   Months later you get a new, better doctor thanks to a referral from friends, and
      for that I will always love them. And she believes fibromyalgia is a real thing
      and for that I will always be grateful to her.

The clothes of characters [14] are doing
a lot of heavy lifting in characterization,
but also in enjoyment. They're aesthetically
pleasing, sure, but to see characters
as themselves, the way they should be?
That's what makes them more alive.
Historical accuracy is great, but
not as great as seeing a colour palate
and shape pair perfectly
to the inner turmoil of a woman on the brink.

I never could sleep in, high-school mornings
in front of a rotating collection of seventies crime-solving
fashion icons: *McMillan & Wife*, *McCloud*, and *Columbo*.
No one did it better. I coveted every piece of clothing
Susan Saint James put on her body. Thrilled with
the regularness of Dennis Weaver's denim.
A trench coat looks best when slopped over Peter Falk,
shoulders slouched from holding up that huge brain.
I don't know if this is my most niche,
humiliating, or best viewing era.

The costumes on *Mad Men* matched
the quality of the show. From 2007 to 2015
I attempted to adorn myself like most
major characters. Taking on each persona
based on needs, wants, and what was availably clean
when I didn't have $4.50 in specific coins
for the laundry machine. Jewel tones, tartans,
wiggle dresses, and swing skirts. YouTube
tutorials tried to teach me updos, but my beehives
were always askew, a hundred visible bobby pins.

14. This has inspired me many times to get into character to leave my apartment.
     Sometimes the only way to get me dressed for work. I'm playing a role. Vintage
     Italian-widow chic. Ms. Frizzle but with way more cleavage. Angry mom who
     just wants to have a liquid lunch. I'm currently in my Mrs. Roper / children's
     entertainer / summer goth era.

When it comes right down to it
I act like I'm a Joan or a Peggy, occasionally
Miss Blankenship, a career worker in service,
but it hurts the most to realize I'm the anti-hero
meanly taking shots at those I love. It was softer
to coldly mock things I wish I understood. Don Draper
walks in and makes assumptions and I hold close
my ways, afraid to give up too much of myself
and show I might also want to be a normie,
not some special genius. Who is? Because I
covet being the main character, it's hard
to believe other people might want to be
in the background. Even harder to consider
putting myself there willingly.

Speaking of coldly mocking, I can do it.
Everyone told me to watch. It was all,
"You gotta see it. It's the best. You're gonna love this."
But *Battlestar Galactica* was a snoozefest.
I could barely pay attention, forced
myself to finish the first season, to be able
to say, "That fucking sucked, dude,"
and move on with the knowledge that I gave
it a solid chance to win me over. And isn't that
what television is supposed to do, episode
after episode, trawl you along, entice
with compelling characters, narrative drive?
This was a long and bad first date. It hurt
my heart to not fall in love with a show.
It's all I ever really want, to be swept up.
Cylons, take me away! They left me floating.
I don't remember anything except
the whole aesthetic looked bad on purpose,
no real style. Maybe I just hate
outer-space drama. Outer-space comedy
I can get behind, but unlike rich teens
or not-so-top models or 1960s ad agencies,
there was nothing that made me forget
about my own life in a world so fantastically
removed from my own. It felt like a waste
of time to not be enthralled. But now
I can say I tried, and so did that show.

Hating shows is almost as fun as loving them. A recommendation for something I hated made me question friendships, taste levels, relationships. But in the end having different tastes means that sometimes I have things just for myself, and I can be mean about the things I don't like for likes on the internet, or to court trolls and scorn from others. Staying social-media healthy with a diet of various interactions, some good, some toxic. But a bad show can be hopeful. In that you can hope for it to improve. That it's going somewhere, hope that it's better than you think it is. [15] Just like Tim Robinson and his Dangerous Nights Crew taught us. If a baby cries in your arms, it could be because they know you used to be a piece of shit. But people can change. You don't have to throw water on steaks, or drink champagne on the beach. You can move slowly, just push your hair back.

15.   And deep down, it's entertaining you somehow, someway!

Being annoying becomes an important part
of our relationship. Me, I mean. I ask you,

"Can you believe *Glee* even existed?
And that I felt like I had to watch

every episode until that guy OD'd
and then TV couldn't even take

away the feeling of emptiness
inside my heart?" And you say nothing.

I should know by now the importance
of lowering my expectations

of entertainment. Not all teen dramas
are created equal. Even musical ones.

Santana drowned and we didn't know yet, watched
on Twitter while they tried to find her body. [16]

16. Do we get too emotionally invested? Not in characters, that's what we're sup-
     posed to do. But in the real people living their lives? An entire industry exists
     to follow and report. But we collectively care and mourn too. Because TV is
     art and art is essential. But TMZ can get fucked. RIP Naya Rivera.

I started watching *Gossip Girl* late, well
not really late, but seven months after it premiered.
Everyone I wanted to be friends with in the M.F.A. [17]
was talking about it. So I got into it,
couldn't look away. Even though I was nothing
like her, I was mimicking Blair Waldorf,
I already owned coloured tights (I worked across
from American Apparel), wore mostly dresses
and skirts. I walked around hoping I could
pout with power. Every week a new event,
parties, launches, album releases, teens
opening a speakeasy. Of course, pretend
I could not resist. The teens looked old
enough but not too old, I was in my twenties
too. I could give myself to caring
about who was from what side of town,
the instant commutes from Brooklyn
to Manhattan that recappers
criticized, but I have still never been
to the East Coast so what do I know about
private schools and Brooklyn and subways,
town cars, galas. I did know about more popular
powerful boys and how they would put
pressure on parts of you that you wanted to ignore,
that being from outside the city was gauche,
that sometimes people would turn on you
for wearing the wrong thing. Teen logic
made a lot of sense.

My new friends were magic.
They were a different fantasy,
smart, interesting, hilarious, bold.
When I started hosting *ANTM* nights
we were making our own event, something
smaller, but that we carried.

17.   Meghan and Claire and Kellee and Sheryda.

Through two apartments I kept up
these Wednesday-night engagements.
Meghan and Claire and Lindsay and Kellee
and Stacey and Laura and Roxan and Sheryda. Whoever
wanted to forget their lives and join in
Tyra's fantasy. Our laughter pierced
through paper-thin apartment walls from 8 p.m.
until we ran out of bang-for-buck wine.

At the height of feeling my feelings,
becoming the person I was going to be,
it really was TV recaps that pushed me
in the direction I needed to go, held
me as I navigated the last years of my twenties.

I ignored the hard parts of life, dove deep
into *Vulture* every morning. An early riser,
NYC recappers were still always there for me
ahead of my tea and cookies. I had to watch
TV just to keep up with the recaps, to find
meaning in the meaning behind the meaning.
It was the most important writing of our time.

As I finished my M.F.A. I realized I would never
write anything as significant, with the readership,
as a 2008 *Gossip Girl* recap on a Tuesday morning.
I know I'd probably never deserve that level of recognition
anyway. Accepting a low-level readership was crucial
to my development as a creative person who couldn't
stop comparing apples and oranges. A poet isn't
a TV writer, isn't a journalist, isn't a recapper.
But a poet can take any of those forms
and manipulate it for their own gains, [18]
say what they want to say while
also saying something about the form itself.
Sure, there are still those heart-sunk days
of wishing people cared about your work, but
you just text those wishes to your many friends. [19]
They are your complaint department.

18. These gains are small and unrelated to muscle acquisition, like, barely even the
    so-called writerly muscle memory.
19. If you don't have many friends, I'm sorry. Also, I am not accepting new friends
    at this time. I am trying to maintain good relationships with the ones I have,
    and I worry about that enough. I'm really glad you bought this book. Or that
    you're reading it. But I really can't have new friends.

Breaking Bad
"Fly"
Season 3, episode 10

A classic bottle episode in an enclosed space, a giant drug-making tank. Well-crafted shots, angles, and a distinct colour palate, a definite intensity. It echoes other episodes emotionally. Jesse and Walt, their father–son vibe, Walt expressing anger at his younger partner. The difference here is the reversal, usual dynamic upended. Jesse tricks Walt into sleep, desperately needed, taking care of him through deceit. The buzzing fly a nuisance. We see the fly, yes. We also see a really arrogant man. A fly could contaminate a batch of illegal drugs, but it's not the worst thing. It's tiny. A minuscule problem, blown up by someone obsessed with himself, his own ego. Perfection is a problem. I think a lot of fans or reviewers see Walter White as a brilliant character. But characters make mistakes. Even ones that seem smart, have advanced degrees, have managed to use a science degree for criminal activity and wealth creation. The lies between two men are imbalanced. One is stealing, a way of escape, in some respect, the other a murderer, in a sense. This episode is visually arresting, but we get the same old song, especially from Jesse's former teacher, who can't seem to learn how to remain a reasonable human being.

Whenever I hear songs from childhood
I'm in the car coming back from the lake
at sunset. We'd begged to stay over
one more night, but no, Dad
had to work or we had to visit family or
a variety of valid other reasons kids
couldn't see as important but understood
they meant something important. It's always
sunset and we're driving around a winding bend
of trees and shrubs and mountains. Lately,
I cry every time I hear a song that generates this newly
invented memory, a composite
of days and car rides and love.
Emotional outpouring.

Every song on *Sports* reminds me of joyful youth.
Singing along to "The Heart of Rock & Roll" with all my little
soul. Dad blasting Huey Lewis and the News recorded from an LP
onto a Maxell for the stereo in the white Corolla.
Light fading as we pass deer grazing in fields,
bears and cubs crossing a yard, wild turkeys
clueless in the middle of the back-road,
two-lane highway. Always riding behind Mom,
my brother behind Dad. Both of us singing,
marking landmarks in our brains. The old church,
the farm with the dilapidated barn, the small lake,
and white horses kicking up dust, the border crossing,
the osprey nest atop the bridge, which meant
we were almost home.

TV doesn't hit the same as a song. Yes, sometimes I cry because of TV, but not because of where or who I was when I watched it. I was always inside the same place, sort of, no movement except the emotional kind. Shows gave themselves a time and place and now I can watch them any time and I'm transported wherever they want me to be, but also to living rooms, bedrooms, thin-carpeted floors, and old futons. Reminders of love, fear, the stress of not knowing what's coming. A song is a few minutes, a season of TV is like a lifetime. I love music, don't get me wrong. It gets me where I need to go, which sometimes is to go fuck myself for liking so much classic rock, and for being a national villain for changing the station any time the Tragically Hip comes on. Music triggers, television transports.

Angelo Badalamenti[20] gave *Twin Peaks*
the ultimate in vibes. Moods created

to accompany characters, soundtrack designed
for drama. I always felt held by the opening theme's

eerie comfort. Gorgeous, but unsettling,
an extremely relatable daily feeling about the world.

Appointments to be told, you're maxed
out on opiates for now. In bed, your

tall frame enveloped in duvets, blankets,
body pillows. Good to know you're there.

Despite this, I waited until you were out to dig
into each episode, scared, alone,

but not. Cooper was himself and not.
Laura Palmer was herself and not.

Who is a fucking tulpa and who's
pretending to be a normal person,

who enjoys always cooking for a man,
who thinks it's not cringeworthy

to take ideas created for *Cosmo*
and place them into their calendars

---

20. Knowing Badalamenti also scored one of my least favourite pieces of media,
National Lampoon's Christmas Vacation, is a very inspiring and beautiful thing.
To see someone you admire sell out for money is beautiful only if they continue
to make what you determine "good art." And that's my take on that.

as if there's something genuine, not
about an ownership? Diane is the force,

I can't look away from her. And yet I feel
the interior dread of adult Audrey. A change.

I'm glad my life has both melodrama and camp,
doesn't mean I'm not always looking for answers

and only finding more holes to hide in. I always
wanted to be an Audrey Horne, until I felt like one.

Bound by my own brain, incapable of figuring
out if I should leave or stay or if I even can.

Maybe I was always Audrey, [21] striving to be a sexpot, all talk no action, afraid to let loose. And we have aged the same, going from young and vibrant to middle-aged and trapped by capitalism and our own brains on the rainy Pacific. Is this what drives me to interrogate my viewing habits? This desire to compare and contrast? To go meta as I escape? When we watch a show, there is a part of us that is assessing who we are and who we aren't, both in relation to television and to our ever-changing selves.

21. "Audrey's Dance" in *Twin Peaks* is such an encapsulation of my teenage self, music that felt dangerous and sexy, while I was chaste and out of my element. A created feeling of adulthood and adolescence at once. Badalamenti was good.

The first time, I remember only
parts of it. Lines of dialogue, every lyric
to the one Zit Remedy song. Swearing
on the CBC, "You were fucking Tessa Campanelli?"
The after-school specialness, because
it was special. A pregnancy, an abortion.
Suicide, AIDS. The second time, I pay attention
to the sweaters, the simplicity of Caitlin's beauty,
the twins' propensity for polka dots, the audacity
of Joey to think he was hot shit. But the third
viewing is when I really notice Liz's bangs
compared to Spike's bangs and how they
represents their traumas. I dwell on Snake
and how he seemed normie, but always
had to witness everyone else's mistakes
and tragedies. Wheels couldn't be sadder
or cooler. Caitlin though, always Caitlin,
involved with everything. The comedy of
Yick and Arthur, fake porno *Swamp Sex Robots*. [22]

I was too young to understand everything
when the show debuted, too old to feel
the true pull of the next generation when those
kids hit the airwaves. On the cusp, born sort of Gen X,
sort of millennial, but identifying
with no generation, and loving the specialness
of being in-between. The cockiness of feeling
free to consume the culture of every other generation
whenever, however I like.

22. If you must know, the first porno I watched was *Bad Mama Jama and the Fat Ladies of the Evening* one evening at a friend's house with a large group of us, because his parents were always out of town.

Another question: Will each generation now get their own *Degrassi*? Will this be how we ground humanity every twenty or thirty years? As long as society exists, from now on, a new group of *Degrassi* youths will shepherd and entertain the children, they will teach them to grow, they will wear the clothes of their time, they will form an encyclopedia that will rival anything in ancient libraries. Cultural markers, and occasionally a rapper will emerge from the cast, but then everyone will be like, "That guy is definitely hitting on underage girls," and hopefully in a future society everyone will be like, "Not cool, man!"

CBC started the series from scratch several times,
and I was ready every time. Watching *Degrassi Junior High*,

then *Degrassi High*, and of course, *Degrassi High: School's Out.*
You seemed less enthusiastic each time. Wandering in

and out of the living room, less and less as each episode,
each rewatch kicked into gear. A rejection of my mode

of viewing choice, but also maybe my coping
strategy. You'd get into baths. Calm your muscles.

Shit. Am I Hannah from *Girls*? [23]

---

23.   I think it can be healthy to consider this thought multiple times throughout a life. Build up self-awareness through this question. I think interrogating this is actually the primary idea behind most self-help, but no one is ready to have that conversation.

I'm on these little trips to feel okay or validated or angry and the remote control and the cursor are my tiny steering wheel. I smell the sweat of a blanket washed infrequently, a depression nest, old clothes, hear the crinkle of Twizzlers and soda fizz as Will McAvoy[24] confesses his love to MacKenzie McHale[25] and I am there and everywhere and nowhere. Sad and happy to be distracted. I am everything. Except together. Which isn't so bad, because there are worse things than enjoying television too much, like enjoying *The Newsroom*.

24. Gross.

25. I watched all *The Newsroom* and I deserve to feel bad about it, as we all do. When we encourage Aaron Sorkin, we make all kin sore. Because it's bad!

Patterns repeat. I refuse to get a cellphone
for years, don't want to be found when I'm out.

I go for drinks after work, call you before I leave.
You say you're making dinner, something simple.

"Sure, I'll be home at eight." I lie. I stay out. I change venues.
I meet up with different friends. I lie. I do shots. A final

vodka soda goes down at 2:15 and I rush home,
as if I'm not a piece of shit for lying, for staying

out with people who only wanted to have fun,
me telling jokes and acting foolish for a small,

appreciative audience. I'm the entertainment,
and I love it. I forget I wanted to be responsible.

This happens so many times, I can't pinpoint individual instances.
Eventually, you stop making dinners. Standing

at the counter is too hard on your legs and back. I should
have eaten more baked-bean burritos, more penne.

You can call it nostalgia but it's not,
really, not every time. Every rerun is not exploratory
fodder for your therapist. Not that
I would know. I've never been to therapy.
I rewatch TV instead. It's therapeutic.

I rewatch shows that make me laugh, because
I can rely on them. Travis or Daniel send memes
they know I'll love. Cynara and Hannah and Meghan
text TikToks when I worry them, with a dark
message, out of nowhere. Amid the levity,
offers. Cynara sends a pizza when I have a cold.
Meghan a beer gift card when I've been laid off.
Hannah a gift basket, a note that says, "We love you
and there's nothing you can do about it."

I keep it on the fridge, surrounded by school photos
of my nieces, postcards, wedding announcements,
and Daniel and I Photoshopped into the La Brea Tar Pits.

Jen shares in my anger. When no one else
wants to be angry, she will. No matter
which emotional pairing I serve her, angry/sad, angry/happy,
angry/jealous. She matches me. Brings me home-baked treats.

Why not return to media that works,
to people that always make life better?

Reruns are a different animal, sturdy and steady like a bear scratching on a tree. Watch a new show? No thank you. That sounds uncomfortable and potentially disruptive to my perfect rerun-watching schedule. To go over and over again the places I've been with the people I love or love to hate or never even really had strong feelings about, but they were there for me and that means something. Cooking shows [26] bore, home renovation is classist bullshit. I am not here to renovate my heart, to add an addition to my soul, to fix the parts of me that seem out of date. [27] HGTV [28] can't compete with the steady stream of familiarity.

26. Do you know what isn't boring and is comfortable? Someone cooking for you. If somehow a TV chef decides to come over with a lasagna, then maybe I'll reconsider. I am so tired of cooking.

27. These also will come back in style and then my wicked, loud, screechy, blaring heart and soul can one again be in vogue.

28. And with HGTV you can't even tell if it's a rerun. Every episode is the same. Oh, that ugly grey laminate flooring in a newer home? Fascinating! Prices are cheaper in cities you don't want to live in, in countries you don't have citizenship for? Astounding.

I am trying to put pieces together before bed,
tie things up neatly, remember

when something happened to a character
and also me, totally different things, but

they felt the same because they happened
the first time I watched that show. I seemed

happy. Even though it might be a lie. Doesn't
matter, it needs to be the memory I click.

"Remember when we ..."
I stop myself from saying more to you.

I keep making the same mistakes. You don't
remember. There is brain fog.

From medications, or from exhaustion.
I ask you to say something nice about me,

so quietly I don't think you hear,
turn out the bedroom light.

Tell Me You Love Me, an ask,
is also the name of a TV show

I found too emotionally
stressful and there were too

many fake dicks. I just wasn't
in the mood for any of it.

When you taught me to download television,
we still had cable, you still had your health.

We gave up on being disappointed. Took control
of our destiny with the Pirate Bay and LimeWire.

Would lie in bed together, laptop on your lap,
you curating our viewing, finally a window into

HBO, premium television at our fingertips. You would
let me rest my head on your chest, Al Swearengen

cocksuckering to his heart's content as we shared
an escape. Beige Army & Navy synthetic-fill comforter,

seventies-orange sheets, pilling, soft and thin. Window open,
letting in the breeze from the bay, us too, living out west.

Streaming, I thought, was supposed to give me a rush, a jolt whenever I needed it. Like syndication always available in some form, but more organized, sleeker. No waiting for a specific time to consume, watching a scrolling screen in black and white and blue, shows and times listed in an endless loop. [29] I could pause to take a shit or get more wine, or snacks, or to scream at the mirrored wall. If that's what I needed. Take a break from the break that is binging. One episode after another keeps my brain occupied. When I finish a series, I spend hours absently going past ever-changing digital posters. For days, I face the screen, unable to click a button. I dream in short bursts that splinter into different narratives. Adventure shows, dating shows on boats, another bullshit story glamorizing a man who murders. Stories I'll never watch, but somehow my subconscious brings them up while I'm asleep.

29. In my youth in Fruitvale, there was always a *TV Times* on the coffee table. A little rectangular newsprint weekly, with shows listed for each day, all day, and even descriptions of the episodes. If there was a rerun, there it was in black and white. Then you could still choose based on your mood: comedy, drama, nature shows, kids' programming. Laid out in print, next to a crossword and a cover article about *Kate & Allie*.

TV Times
Saturday 8:00 p.m.

Channel 6
Hold the Phone
"Seagulls?!"

After a disastrous workday in
retail, Dina struggles with public
transit on her commute home.
An encounter with a disgruntled
passenger causes her to get off the
bus and walk home, finding herself
on a journey of self-discovery, and
lots of dog, bird, and rat shit.

Channel 12
Happy Hour
"Aperol Spritz"

Dina, Daniel, and Roxan meet
at Earls on Robson to discover
they've changed the evening
happy-hour menu and their
favourite server has been sacked.
While sampling the new menu,
they devise a plan to get the
server's job back and convince
Earls to bring back mini pizzas.

Channel 18
Home Bodies
"Episode 10"

In the season 38 finale, Dina stays
up late watching a marathon of
Ugly Betty. She wakes up and
finds herself in the Suarez home as
Betty herself. When she turns on
the television, there is a version of
herself in the screen, staring at a
screen. Unsure of how to navigate
her way around Queens to get
to Manhattan and get to work so
the character doesn't lose her job,
she uses her television-watching
knowledge to guide her. But can
she figure out how to get back to
her real world on the other side of
the screen?

Channel 29
The Nature of Wings
"Lost Lagoon"

On a mental-health walk around
Lost Lagoon, Dina sort of explains
the types of ducks that live there,
but unprofessionally keeps having
to look things up on her phone to
make sure she's not lying.

During the pandemic I started to panic
there would be no new TV. I hoarded shows,
saved them up, eked them out. I knew
people were wasting their time with
toilet paper and cold-and-flu meds. At home,
their eyes glued to *Tiger King*. [30] Huge mistakes.
My enjoyment of life needed to be meted out in doses
in case my worst fears came true. Always something
waiting in reserve. Just in case. In case I lost it
and needed something fresh to me. I'd lie awake
at night worried HBO would stop existing, worried
that Netflix would become YouTube. Streaming
only from people's homes with their ring lights,
their families shooting for them in the background.
I wanted televised perfection. If I'm living an imperfect
existence, technically a mess, when using tech,
when technically making a mess. I like when we're all
watching the same show. It makes me feel less alone
to read your tweets about *Mare of Easttown, The White Lotus,
Succession, Yellowjackets, Bridgerton, Abbott Elementary.*

30. Fuck everyone who is mean to tigers or any big cats, I truly hope you all fall
     into a pit full of cougars.

Flipping channels was the eighties and nineties version of scrolling through new releases you don't give a shit about. Algorithms don't even work properly. Netflix, please stop recommending I watch *The Ranch*. I am not here for Ashton in any capacity. Who knows me? Not even television. Not even streaming services. I miss being able to click away when I saw something I didn't like. Pass the clicker! But when you care about other people, you have to look at things you don't like head on. A lot. Sometimes you can glance to the side, catch it in the periphery. Mostly, it's not that easy. Physical health and mental health, how does someone look sick. My teeth have always caused me problems. I have them removed and replaced, crowns and implants. Hemorrhoids too, bothered me for years, but a very nice doctor banded them away. They were likely caused by stress, and I felt because I was the one who brought them into being with my stress levels, I had to keep them.

At work I try not to show the bosses exactly
how much I think they're not smart or capable but
like a fifties TV housewife I can't hide my true emotions
from my overactive face. These expressions are explosions.
What if some days it's too depressing to be at home
or at work and it's a pandemic and all the bars are closed
and you think coffee-shop culture is toxic, and it's raining
and owning rain gear also makes you depressed because
it's so hideous and lifeless and what do you do?

You're so tall, but emerging from the steam in your navy
robe you look like a child in trouble. Head down,

I don't have spells that really heal. Sabrina
Spellman always has to sacrifice something,

but I'm holding on, and know the rule:
I can't fall asleep on watch, but I'm so tired.

You have physical pain, but don't look sick,
I know the meaner people in my life

assume I lie when I say you have trouble walking,
that travel isn't pleasure when you are supposed

to behave while visiting with people, pretend
everything is fine, look at historical monuments. Never be honest.

Rerun. I keep making the same mistakes. Acting like
it's my personality, but that's disappointing because

I'd rather have a better personality. I chase a drama
with a comedy to help me sleep. But then

my dreams are wildly confusing. I tell you
about a dream I had, where you were running

on the beach. I devastate you, dream you
able to move quickly, get to the beach,

and still have the energy to move. I remember
it's recurring. I stop telling you about my dreams.

I got behind on my taxes for years
but somehow managed to find time to watch
eight seasons of a show I don't remember.
For years, whenever I tried to take out a T4, I felt
as if I'd fallen off a piece of eighties schoolyard
play equipment into a pit of pebbles.
My shame is a weed that blooms constantly,
and the only way to slow it down is to download
an entire season of a show full of irresponsible
characters. Multiple shows, every show. I need
to see people misbehaving, I cannot watch
responsible adults right now. I need to feel seen.

Difficult People, You're the Worst, Happy
Endings, Party Down. Half-hours filled
with mistakes and small, slow changes,
barely perceptible. Extremely realistic
human experiences. When Julie and Billy
create fake strikes to enjoy popular
restaurants and theatres, I understand the impulse,
I too want things I can't and shouldn't have.

Selfishly I pine for entertainment, crave experiences
that might hurt others, for flickers of fun,
a surge of joy, serotonin rising. The fights on
You're the Worst cut to the bone of human pain. Cheating,
stealing, scamming, lying. These cheap fictionalized
releases give me bouts of strength to move
through the monotony of my, mostly, obedient life.
Every episode of *Happy Endings* has one problematic
moment, amid the goofs, and I cherish these like
plastic childhood keepsakes. I have watched some
Party Down scenes four dozen times. Service workers
fucking around on the job is the most relatable. Professionalism
when you're expected to serve is a failure. Don't do too good
of a job. Smash a tray of cocktails, eat the client's food.
Ids gone wild, and no one even has to take their top off
if they don't want to.

But in front of the TV, I could entertain myself for hours
drawing my own characters, and scenes
on construction paper, in notebooks. Barbie's
overly dramatic adventures inspired by sick days
with my mom, watching *Another World*
or *General Hospital.* The whole Barbie gang
on a road trip in their second-hand RV,
looking for fossils. Midge and Barbie, long lost twins.
Belinda in a coma on the Rockers' pool party tour
because she was pushed into the empty hot tub by Ken.
Ken, always disposable, the least interesting character.
Eventually I left him in the back of the closet, alone. No more
adventures for his plastic follicles.

My uncle built me a Barbie house that fit perfectly
into my closet. One floor, like a multi-cam sitcom
apartment, bedroom, living room, kitchen. Just like
every one-bedroom apartment I've lived in.
When I played I never thought about growing up
to a life with a nuclear family and a huge house.
My Barbies drove a shiny pink Corvette.
Their lives were rich and dramatic, fun and tragic.
I don't believe in manifestation. But in some way,
maybe the way I played manifested a mode of living.
My Barbies had a standard poodle and I've never
lived in an apartment where it was legal to have a pet.

Stories about me crying start
with television. Dino Flintstone
ran away and I didn't stick around
to find out he returned. Sobbed
and ran and hid under my bed.
Dad got home from work and Mom
showed him tiny legs protruding,
laughed, because that's so adorable,
she cares about the fictional. [31]
I can't say I don't agree.

31. My parents are actually the best and I think this is a cute and funny story, so
    don't think you're getting parental trauma shit in this book. This is not that
    book.

There are unanswerable questions [32] throughout a life. One is why would a brontosaurus leave home when he was so loved? One little incident to turn a loyal dino-dog into a fragile boy. And why would a man yell at his loyal dino-dog? An early lesson in male aggression, a man's desire to be right and righteous and impulsive. The brontosaurus was rightfully jealous of a baby. Babies dominate time and attention and nothing is more relatable than baby envy. Gets in the way of the ones we love. It felt cruel at the time, for this perfect, very good boy to run away. I now know story means creating issues, causes and effects of misunderstandings the basis of sitcom conflicts. More dramatic than real-life conflicts. Those seethe, prickle under the surface, get pushed down because it's not always the right time to make people you love uncomfortable.

32. Other questions: Why do some people get sick and why do some people have two lazy eyes and what is the point of a structure for a poetry book when trying to harness chaos is just, like, the way of the world, man?

I daydream scenarios. Walk into the boss's office,
quit because I got my dream job, get discovered
hosting a poetry event and given my own talk show.
I sell a book to a customer, make the best joke ever told,
and they're a producer who hires me on the spot
to create my own sitcom. I tweet something so profound
that my phone literally explodes from offers,
helicopters drop bagfuls of money at my doorstep, rich, cool
people courting me for projects, to consult my wisdom, to be
on the cover of *Cool Brilliant Girl Magazine*.

When I think of Amy Jellicoe, I think of someone
who wants to be admired and is learning that it doesn't

matter. To just do the work and one day change will come.
Learning that anger never really leaves you, it changes

form and melds with other emotions: fear, sadness, jealousy,
glee. It can be pulled out like a multitool. Sleeping with your

married boss is a cliché that always teaches the same lesson.
Men in power will demote and demean. She learns that pastels

are power colours, not to be underestimated as weak
femininity. They burn. I learned this too late too.

Lavender and baby blue repel the gaze of men, create
a front for intelligence. When I dress like a pastry,

frothy, poofed skirt in lemon-pith yellow, frilled pink blouse,
my boss doesn't think I'll scheme to get him fired.

You wear only black now. Like a goth, or a villain,
or a goth villain. It's striking on you. You grow a beard.

It took a long time for me to figure out that things come and go. I always want more, but never want to give anything up. A greed. Constant. It's worse when there's nothing on because I feel less lonely if I cry in front of the TV. It's worse when I forget I'm not always going to be slumped down. It's worse when I forget I love television, when I remember to watch it with excitement, with love, with a childish enthusiasm. It's better when I remember *Succession* is coming back soon. But worse when someone points out it's the final season. Things end and we can revisit them in some way, but it's never the same and neither are we.

Things changed. People domesticated.
I resisted. Even though I'd been espoused

to you for over twenty years. It just didn't mean
as much as a full life, which our relationship

was one part of. Not the whole part.
I am not that person. So imperfect.

I could never say my spouse was my best friend.
I already had one. It's fine for other people

to feel that way. Even though no matter
how you say it, that sounds bitchy.

"Oh, of course, oh my god, yeah, like,
it's fine for you. It's just not for me."

No, I pushed away from rooting myself
to a domestic partner only, and yet

I was too boring to be poly, too disorganized
for an affair. And mostly, wasn't even

interested. I wanted friendship. I craved
doing stuff. Not being home. Cocktails

on patios and road trips, dates
to shop, scream, watch. With

people outside my relationship,
friends. But people wanted to hunker,

the thing I feared more than having
to face my financial realties came true,

clichés of nights alone because no one
wanted to go out. I stayed up late,

imagining the dull evenings of steaks
and home-improvement shows, dreams

of dogs one day, more reasons to stay in
and not see me. I felt thirteen, immature

and ruined. Listened to Mazzy Star and stared
into the moon. Raged to riot grrrls, held my head

under a stream of melting ice cream, slept with
chocolate bars, stuffed otters, a night light. Then

I discovered soft teen comedies. Throwbacks,
laugh tracks, nineties TV stars now the parents,

Kelly from *Saved by the Bell* is the tightly wound
mother on *Alexa & Katie*,[33] *Sabrina the Teenage Witch*

now matriarch of the family in *No Good Nick*.
They've grown and own homes, here I am, child-free,

renting a one-bedroom apartment, wondering
what the word "career" means. But these shows,

grounding narratives in *Teen Beat* nostalgia,
and that burst in the chest, not of romantic

love but the deep friendships that we felt
would break us open into new people

because they did. The thrill of loyalty,
because our love was paramount, beat

33.   I cried during most episodes of this show.

harder in our chests than cheap crushes,
boners bored into thighs, school dances we wished away.

I binged. Best friends shave their heads together
because one has cancer. A teen scam artist

pulls together a family and, instead of scamming
them, finds she loves them in return.

When I go online and watch TV, I compare.
See old friends and know to them I am a villain somehow.
Or worse not even worth remembering. I tell myself
stories of what I've done to harm them, but I'll never know.
Just like how a character in a good show might never know
what they did to harm. I had a dream
I was caring for Niles Crane. Cradling him
like a baby, wiping his brow with a wash cloth
of better quality than my own clothes. I wake up
and think about Frasier Crane. Imagine
someone has to choose between Patricia Clarkson
and Jean Smart? Lucky. I dumped so many dating shows.
I never made it to *The Bachelor*. *5th Wheel, Blind Date,*
I watched them daily while cooking dinner.

Too much and not enough me. I feel contradictions
crashing into me. At work. I feel it crashing into me.
I have meetings. Other jobs, syllabuses to write
and unfinished drafts waiting for me. I have podcasts
to record and I think about quitting this job as it crashes into me.
I whisper, "It's crashing into me" as I walk past the fiction section
full of books by people who have different and similar lives
to mine. I feel it crashing into me. I think about quitting. I don't.
I can't. I have half-finished dental work. I have to keep doing it all
until I find myself a Niles Crane to pay for me to exist. Jkjkjk.
I feel it crashing into me and I think about farting into my couch
later, after work, 80-percent-covered massage therapy,
a fast-grilled cheese sandwich on a sloppy frying pan. Me
farting into the couch watching *Frasier*, rich with money
and education, failing to connect to women who exist only
for him to maybe connect to. I pretend my plush mammoth
is a real pet. Like Eddie. I pet her. Goldie the Gold-Digging
Mammoth. I pet the felt lion, the plush otters, my own head,
and the fur of my arm, wrap myself in the white tiger–leopard
blanket. Nest. I feel myself crashing into sleep.

On the thirtieth anniversary of *Twin Peaks*
I'm thinking about anniversaries,

how we don't really have one,
and never celebrate anything.

It's fine to wish for a lack
of sentiment. I want daily care,

though sure, I'm more of a big party
planner, but that's not what I'm gonna

get now. Or ever. Other friends
mark date-iversaries, actively

call time spent together Date Night.
I scoff because I'd rather be lost

in a surreal lodge, in the sheen
of a cherry in a perfect slice of pie.

The things we do to normalize
the way we live are thrown out

if there are any anomalies, like
looking at the world through

purple-tinted glasses. When *The Return*
came on, I had rewatched and was ready.

Your presence in our home
is grounding even though

you're always struggling. I feel
less scared of the unknown,

even though with you there
are always unknowns.

You're in the middle of pain flares,
balancing drugs, creams, injections.

In reality, I visit Daniel in the place TV is made.
And even though I still think it's magic in a box,
I know people work to create, building sets, writing,
arguing, being at the mercy of executives like the rest
of us. Daniel takes me to Universal Studios. First thing
we see is a *Days of Our Lives* fan convention, a flashback
to the soap opera of my undergrad days. More feelings.
Marlena was possessed by the devil and Princess Gina
was Hope and I was in a dorm living away for the first time
like the country bumpkin I am. Thrilled to talk soap gossip
with the floor. I know none of the actors appearing, as far
as I know, none of them were possessed by the devil,
had amnesia, or thought they were European royalty. I bet one
had a secret twin. On the tram tour the sets are visible,
the underpaid tour host tells us what is filming, all shows
I don't watch. This is what happens when you cancel cable,
you become unaware of basic broadcasting.

I get fed up with you. I'm not a martyr,
never said I was. I need breaks from

sharing space, from feeling like I'm helping you.
But maybe I'm not, or maybe I'm not doing

it right. But I am my own person and so are you.
We are not some single entity, a creature from

The Twilight Zone or something we learn
a lesson from on *Black Mirror*.

I need breaks from you. And I won't
apologize for it. Even if I should.

I ignore your tears and pain because I can
only lie beside you on the hardwood so long,

without you responding, without attention.
I like attention. I like praise. I can be patient,

but I can also be petty. I go to bed without
saying a word because I think it's better

than saying, "I am fucking over this shit!"
Or even, "It's okay, honey, you just do

what you need to do." I should've gone
to sleep earlier anyway. So tired. Woke up

at 5 a.m. and now it's 1 a.m. Mostly, I don't
want to be disruptive. You breathe heavily.

Detached from traditional viewing, we exit the tram
and find nostalgia in Springfield. "Life-size" *Simpsons*
figures brightly pop and I feel a catch in my throat. [34] Did anything
ever mean so much to me as when I would sit down with my family
to watch this animated one? To see their imperfect humanity
and impeccable jokes? We drink Duff Beer and ride the ride
inspired, slight nausea hits as we land and I don't know if it's
because I'm giddy or too full of draft. I insist we pose with
Milhouse and Barney. The underdogs, side characters with rich
lives who never get to be on top. I play a game guaranteed to win
a prize and Daniel says we take the Itchy doll, a sadistic mouse
who tortures and wins every time. He insists we go
in *The Walking Dead* haunted house because he loves
to be scared. But to him it's tame, even though I hate
jump scares and use him as a shield until we're through.

34. Maybe I was wrong before and there is something that TV can trigger, but
only if you're not watching it, exposed to a commercial aspect of that show.
An object, a T-shirt, a fanny pack, branded bubble gum. Completely immers-
ing yourself in a simulation that replicates all the places from your childhood
television viewing is going to cause you to feel a shit ton of nostalgia and well
up with emotion. How could that not mess someone up, you know?

I can play other characters outside the home.
Sassy co-worker, summer babe catcalled

in the street, righteous lady shouting
at drivers for almost hitting pedestrians

in crosswalks. Fun-loving, pseudo-manic,
middle-aged pixie-woman. The multitudes

we are supposed to contain. So much narrative
in my brain, makes me create scenarios, attempts

to draw connections and conclusions, tie things
up like a writer might. But it's hack. The mess is key.

If I was on a TV show, I imagine fans on Twitter
would obsess over the small scar below my lip, [35]

or my two lazy eyes. [36] The fan illustrations [37] would
highlight the things I've always felt weird about.

My eyes are both lazy, especially when I'm tired.
But one always comes in clutch to compensate

for the tired one. They take care of each other. Share.
A beautiful, metaphorical cliché right in my own face.

35.   I got this scar from a T-bar slapping me in the face when I was fourteen. This
      was the last time I went skiing. I was also being treated for facial warts at this
      time. If you really want to picture me as a teenager.
36.   I found out after living my entire life thinking I had only one lazy eye that they
      are both lazy. I want to thank that optometrist for illuminating my eyeballs and
      their whole deal.
37.   The way I see fans on Twitter or TikTok babygirl-ing Netflix murderers (like Joe
      Goldberg on *You*) and their pouty lips, or teen stars and gap teeth, or televised
      billionaires and their dysfunctions. I'm not saying these are all equal, but fan
      vibes are the same.

I'm not here to demonize a character or myself or you. I'm not here to push us into little boxes. We are as varied as the casts of *Saturday Night Live* for almost fifty years. A personality marker I feel can be accurately applied to at least 90 percent of people.

QUIZ

Which *SNL* Cast Member Are You?

1. **You find an injured dog by the side of the road. You:**
   a. Kick them into the woods and tell them to, "Get outta here, you hear me?!"
   b. Wait for someone to drive by to help.
   c. Wrap it in your coat and carry the beast to the nearest vet.
   d. Wrap it in your coat and carry the beast to the nearest vet, find out if the dog has an owner, and if not, then adopt it and nurse it back to health.

2. **You're confronted with a ghost. You:**
   a. Kick them into the woods and tell them to, "Get outta here, you hear me?!"
   b. Ask the ghost if they're interested in a franchising opportunity. Not a restaurant, but maybe a Disneyland ride adaptation.
   c. Offer the ghost refreshments, realize they probably can't imbibe, and then beat yourself up about it.
   d. Befriend the ghost and introduce them to all your other friends.

3. **You think about your inner child and you want to:**
   a. Kick them into the woods and tell them to, "Get outta here, you hear me?!"
   b. Buy them some really nice toys, set them up in a beautiful room, and let them enjoy an uninterrupted day of playing.
   c. Wrap them in a big hug, walk them to the ocean, and watch the waves lap at the shore.
   d. Throw them a party for no good reason, with everything they love to eat, activities that make them happy, and of course, all their favourite people.

4. **In moments of self-doubt, your reaction is to:**
   a. Kick it into the woods and tell it to, "Get outta here, you hear me?!"
   b. Find something you're good at and do that to build back your confidence.
   c. Do a bump and take a shot.
   d. Revel in the reality of your life, the support you have from loved ones. Also, you put on something very cute and comfortable and remember that sometimes we all suck, and that's the most normal thing in the known universe.

Results

Mostly a's: You are Chevy Chase. A real overrated, boring piece of shit.

Mostly b's: You are Eddie Murphy. You are a steady force, always ready to show up, but sometimes you make mistakes. Like, maybe you wore too many fat suits.

Mostly c's: You are Chris Farley. There is an uneasiness to you, and a wild nature, but also a gentleness.

Mostly d's: You are Kristen Wiig. Everyone likes you and you are smart and fun and boy oh boy people really wish they were your friend.

You and I are varied too. We are Sam & Diane,
but we're not. I'm a bit annoying, you quit drinking.

Because you're on so many medications. I take
some too. You watch YouTube wresting podcasts,

I pair a canned cocktail with dinner and my
chosen viewing for the evening. You obsess

over *Tears of the Kingdom* advance video reviews
and I watch TikToks of flocked animals

from my youth who have the most unhinged
soap-opera adventures. To feel alive.

Nothing big or magical ever happens.
Like contemporary sadcoms there is realism.
Good moments mocking bad bosses at work
to pass the time, improve morale. Meeting
Cynara to run errands on the weekend, Rox
for happy hour at Earls, texting Daniel all day
about everything, venting with Jen. To cope.
Big is rare. Magical is rare. It's so rare,
it's almost unbelievable that any magic exists.
Less believable than the time jumping in *Outlander*.

I wish I could crawl into the box
less boxlike now than when wee

when I was too scared to watch
the movie about the kid getting sucked

into the television. It's warm, pulses,
and I would love to hollow out

an old wood-panelled television,
make a tiny bed for myself in there.

I don't even like enclosed spaces,
want to be free, but that's what

it does to me. Frees me from thoughts
that I don't want to have. Pushes

away the real personal and lets
me get personal with those

in the box. Silk scarves, stuffed
otters, fat pillows squished

into my cheek. Dark glass instead
of the bulky old tube. A small

hanging light above. To keep
me lit, keep me lighter.

I can't imagine ever not feeling
like a cartoon anvil will slam
me into the earth.

You are sleeping so much,
I barely see you.
And when I do, your face is telling.

I type long blue boxes of text
into my phone. Revise. Send shortened versions
to Daniel, to Rox, to Jen, to Meghan, to Cynara, to Hannah.
They are all aware of me having feelings.

When you're usually entertaining, high-energy,
extroverted, you assume there are assumptions
about how you're supposed to be.

I rewatch *I Think You Should Leave*
for the tenth or fifteenth time. It still feels like the first time. [38]
I still wonder how many degrees of separation I am
from Patti Harrison and Tim Robinson and Sam Richardson.
Would they even like me? Would they be my friends?
I wonder if having "son" as part of a surname makes a creator
a comedic genius even though I object to the word "genius"
but it would be good to know if that is why I'm not
more successful, more of a genius, more desirable,
more exciting to people with money to let me
make art. Make a better life. Be better.

38.   But also full of more nuances and I anticipate the dopamine.

What an absolute bitch! is a phrase that runs through my head constantly. Positively, and negatively. Television never tells me to stop, never says I'm too much, never shushes me or asks me to slow my roll. It's not possible to live under capitalism and not have some level of greed. For attention, for praise. A selfish desire to always be enthralled. I had.to practise being alone without a screen. I had to train to be calm. I had to figure out how to relax. Capitalism wants us to mimic a doll house, nuclear families, nothing queer about our love, the way we interact. Not falling over backwards for your spouse, even if they're disabled. The paths we make aren't based solely on choices. Sometimes we have fewer choices. Instead of television I could travel, but I'd have to spend less money at home, where I live, to find moments of elation for a brief period of time. I'd rather see my life where I live, with the people I love, be less of a piece of shit than spend money exploring the world. You come back to dirty dishes and mountains of work. [39]

39. Everything connected to traditional marriage and nuclear families is pretty damaging. Think about it. Like, we deserve better! Everyone needs to get their head out of *Leave It to Beaver*'s ass! Community care is gonna get us through life and not some lies about who should be important to us and our existence in the world.

Calculations of how much television I have watched
instead of doing literally anything else. While sick[40]
or while healthy, letting stories take up my time. Tying
together the threads of television with the threads of my life.
Admitting to myself that the feeling of longing
and to be wanted is something I yearn for. Not always,
but I do. On a rainy Sunday afternoon, I let myself indulge
in the nostalgic melancholy I would hate if it was onscreen.
But alone in yesterday's pajamas, haven't left my apartment
for forty-eight hours just because it feels like the kind of effort
I'd rather reserve for caring about what Philip and Elizabeth
will get up to on *The Americans*. They have real problems!
Soviet spies, hiding wigs all over town. I'm jealous of their ability
to change appearances so quickly. Some days it takes two hours
to select an acceptable outfit. But today I think about Sunday
afternoons and evenings at Nonno and Nonna's house,
cozy in their kitchen, waiting while she cooked. And he
could let us play with his novelty liquor bottles. A ballerina in gin.
A lemon floating in vodka. Plums suspended in liqueur. The TV
always on, her companion while she cooked. And the news playing
before we ate. And *The Wonderful World of Disney*
when we finished, maybe during dessert. I have never
felt so cared for. I know I didn't always appreciate the ritual.
The smells. The house. When I dream of my hometown,
most often my dreams are set in their house.

40. Sometimes, when I'm burned out, I imagine getting very sick just so I can stay
    home and watch television, needing a more legitimate reason to rest. Which is
    such a darkly distressing reality of the contemporary grind-culture workplace.
    But as a kid, watching *The Price Is Right* did always seem to be the cure.

Like a rerun of my life. I know there were times I sat there
in my chair, waiting for fried zucchini and flowers, that I let
my tiny brain go into dread. Once I worried that I had kissed
the boy across the street in the weeds where now
there is a very ugly house. I thought my family would hate me
if they knew that I had done it. I couldn't get it out of my head.
That every mistake I made would cause hate, disgust, disownment.
But I was loved. I was cared for. I was. My brain was a bastard.

Driving you to a medical appointment
in the suburbs, I feel pressure,

panic in the driver's seat,
almost cut off the HandyDART.

My hands shake, I mutter about
what a piece of shit I am, fuck, fuck, fuck.

You speak to me calmly, nervous,
I can hear it in your voice.

"It's allowed," you say. "You're allowed
to feel bad," you say. You say, "Ask

for help." Even though you hate
asking, and know it doesn't mean

you're getting help, or quality help,
or relief. You encourage me.

To seek the same, or better.
You want better for me.

Ricki, Sally, Oprah, Donahue. They wanted us to be entertained, but there was always a premise of learning. Teaching us lessons about life, about human connectivity. They had "experts" on and we all watched and were supposed to trust. Because if you get a car and you get a car and you get a car and you get a feel-good story and you get a feel-good story and you get a feel-good story then if you get a mental-health revelation and you get a mental-health revelation and you get a mental-health revelation there is hope for us all. On a talk show, regular people ask for personal advice on television, surrounded by an audience, and they get an immediate response, and it might even help, or at least it might seem like it does. "How do I improve my physical health?" "How can I get my children to stop being goth?" "How do I tell my disabled boyfriend not to do everything in bed, not sex stuff, but eating, scratching lottery tickets, drinking Slurpees, without seeming like an absolute monster?"

I can sleep if I spend three hours with
TV teens in twenty-two-minute increments. Every

new fantasy feels real. I know I say it
all the time. But they're my friends too.

That comfort started early. Screens
as companions. Not that I didn't have friends,

I obviously had a lot of friends, okay.
Like, now, I also have a lot of friends. [41]

But I am greedy. Love to consume,
crave noise, colour, visuals. Theme

of my life: can't be still, enjoy silence,
which is funny since those are both

annoying traits. Some part of me
undiagnosed, I think, with some

kind of mental-health issue. Need
to never be still, always entertained

or entertaining. To be the audience,
or need an audience. Engagement.

Your ability to be alone for long periods of time
impresses me, and makes me homesick

for that time and place when you saw
me, and I was a comfort.

41. Not to harp on this, but I really do have a lot of friends. Like, they're the best,
      and I'm sure you're great too, and if you want a lot of friends I hope you find
      them, and if not can I recommend watching some television?

All these stories about me crying. For months,
I can barely stop doing it, any time I'm alone.

Jen tells me it's always okay to cry. But also
always okay to want to feel better. Even though
she's an expert in reality dating shows, I would still
trust her with the lives of everyone I love. Our viewing
overlaps are small, but our overlaps on views of the world
are more vast.

I walk into the London Drugs I used to go to
and they're renovating. My throat is dry
but I don't get an overpriced kombucha,
I stuff the toilet paper and cola candies I've been carrying
into the summer-clearance shelves and run out of the store.

The thematic threads are winding around me.
My brain is a pinball machine, the chain store
moved the ice cream, it's warm out, and I'm
devastated instead of delighted. Everything
is improving but not me. I am the same, but worse.

I sob the whole walk home, like I'm giving
my best Claire Danes in *Homeland*, season 1.

Sometimes I think there isn't enough television in the world to fill me up, but I try. The end of a series detrimental to self-care. Watching the credits, I hope for a moment of acceptance, but instead get tremors of anxiety. Why can't I live in front of the screen forever? How dare Diane Lockhart leave me for another week? I work so many jobs, so much. I dream about getting the flu again so I can lay a flat sheet on the couch, sip apple juice and sparkling water, watch TV for three weeks straight. An excuse to not have to push myself to be productive seven days a week. Thinking again about how I've never seen *Grey's Anatomy*. Though, doing the math, it would take me three flu cycles to get through every episode. I have this fantasy that I spend and give away all my money just to see what happens next. Not because I want to die, though sometimes I do, but because nothing makes me feel worse than knowing I have money I don't think I deserve, that I don't have money, that I don't know how to be an adult with money, and that I'm to blame for not making enough money to keep up with how much money it costs to be alive. [42] And to know so many have so little money and I just ordered so many candles online so I can sit in the dark and watch TV.

42. Money. What a fucker.

TV asks so little of me. It's hard not to love that,
admire the restraint. To just let me enjoy myself

or turn it off at my whim. I water the plants
from hot-water bottles, guilt from using so many

resources, but your body needs relief, and who am I
to say you don't need to use ten litres a day?

I drown the spider plant, and all their babies.
Vow to keep the others safe, use an app to gauge

their water needs. You bought all these when we moved in,
a low-impact activity that now is beyond your daily capacity.

I devote myself to eighteen pots of dirt, stems, and leaves.
Like the greenhouse in *Weeds*. I heard there is a reality show

about competitive pruning. I vow too never to watch it.
These calm reality shows do nothing for me. I do not

want to calm down. I want to feel something
burst through all my internal organs, sear my guts.

I can't be happy for people who quit their day jobs
to pursue their creative dreams. Not if they own a house,

not if they own a car, not if they have a husband paying,
benefits to cover their rotten-tooth emergencies and bad

skin. What's at stake? If the only discomfort
someone experiences is related to their art creation

and all the time they have to do it, then I have
to hate them. Being a mean bitch is hard work.

I only have confidence about impractical
activities. And a little left over for manual

labour. I will dig a ditch, but I never want
to have proficient knife skills.

Wow. I'm depressed. I can admit it. I've never been to therapy and only saw two and a half seasons of *The Sopranos*. Yes, I know who Dr. Melfi is. No, I don't know how to take care of myself. When you live with someone with depression you don't want to be rude, take away their identity by having the same issue. I told myself this. Over and over. Pull the twee cat-head sheets up high and hide instead. We can't both be the patients, one of us has to be the Frasier Crane. Except we live in a one-bedroom apartment with no view and no dog and we aren't pompous enough to think we deserve to help ourselves. One has to be of use, just has to be. Sometimes I think I'm too weak to have a full-on breakdown. But of course, that's not how it works. I feel like I'm having outbursts all the time, but I still hold so much back. It sucks to know I'm failing at responsibly dealing with my emotions and also at not expressing them. When is the right time to tell people in your life you're watching TV constantly because you can't bear to worry every other spare moment? The concept of free time presupposes that watching TV isn't an important activity that uses time like other tasks: toothbrushing, grocery shopping, contemplating the right time to tell someone about your television-viewing habits. Confess what and how much you're watching.

I can't use magic to cure you, ease pain with spells,
clairvoyance to understand why the fuck

some people's bodies behave badly
for no reason. But I can draw baths, sprinkle

Epsom salts, and cradle your face when you want
to not be alive anymore. I can ask what else

I can add to the tub, and when you say a plugged-in
iron, I can laugh because I know that's what you

want me to do and because it's funny.
I don't have werewolves or fairies advising me on who

is best to talk to when someone seems cursed.
I can watch TV and wait for something better

to happen in real life.

Vampires have opposite schedules
and they make it work. You work

graveyard shift and I'm depressed
and you're depressed. We have

twin hot-water bottles, for when your back aches
and my uterus punches me from inside,

in bed before I leave for work, and you get home,
bodies pulsing with need, for relief.

So I finally take SSRIs, I go back to the mob. Classic.
Invested in how hard it was gonna be on Tony
to wack Pussy. Crying over ducks. Crying over *ducks*.

I tweet my feelings about *The Sopranos* in a long thread,
and text Meghan every time I get excited about a plot
shift I didn't see coming, my reaction to Carmela's hair,
Adriana's style choices. I search animal-print "catsuits" online.
I tell Daniel we need matching tracksuits to tour
our books whenever we finish them.

Weeks later, at dawn, I get up and walk the lagoon,
the ducklings so big. I remember the panic,
how recently I couldn't handle
the way I had to be sad about their growth
while I stayed the same, haunted by the inability
to change.

But I had changed. I'd grown older. I walked
around an artificial lagoon in search of ducks
because it brought calm to my heart. I asked
my terrible doctor for help, even though
the way he spoke to me always made me wish
I could just send him an eloquent email instead.

I made a start.

I finished *The Sopranos* and they definitely
didn't get shot up in that diner. Life just,
shit just, went on, and on, and on.

Being newly diagnosed with depression can make a person unbearable. Because you see stupid depression shit in every stupid thing. Am I a character? Or am I really just working things out, out loud, to try and understand myself? A character constantly joking, to be the clown, to make everyone else feel better when they cry alone. Classic clichés that I have lived. Try me. I should have set up a camera to record myself years ago, but would it then have just become a performance, or would I have forgotten about the cameras? Downplaying my desires is something I do that makes me feel safe, but in fact is probably diminishing me. But also, enough disappointments. Wondering if I want a different life, if it's too late for me to find the level of appreciation and devotion I crave. Do I want that? [43] Have I been lying to myself? [44] And what have I been lying to myself about? [45]

43. I want something.
44. Always lying to myself a little bit. That's how I keep some level of hope.
45. That I look good, or look bad, or that I deserve notoriety, or I deserve nothing. And I dare you to tell me you don't lie to yourself. You're doing it! Don't lie to me right now!

I take Sara out for treats
on Valentine's Day and we talk
brain drugs over brioche doughnuts
and spendy sodas.

For no reason
Jen texts me, "I LOVE YOU"
and I text her back,
"I LOVE YOU TOO."

Meghan and I swim
at the outdoor pool,
quote Kendall, "I'm the eldest boy!"
from the *Succession* finale.

Cynara and Jessica and Hannah
share selfies in the group chat.
Approval for our not-so-little treats
purchased online.

Roxan and I plant tomatoes,
mourn the loss of our stolen,
cheap-metal garden rooster,
no longer playing saxophone in beds of red lettuce.

A nice little mix of weekly releases and full-season drops. A healthy balance. A diet of comedies and dramas and whatever we're calling this new form of docuseries that are somehow both gentle and emotionally hard-hitting. Living in the sweet spot.

I go to the beach with Meghan and Hannah and Roxan. We spread belongings out on blankets, supplies we need for the day: our tiny coolers, big hats, water bottles rattling with ice cubes. We read books in tiny bursts between conversations, plunge into the waves. We make slow-mo videos, running in the sand, splashing like toddlers. Remember the era of *Baywatch*, but not the specific content. We post online, then later in bed I leave comments, emojis. Hearts and waves, inside jokes. Actual perfect visuals from a perfect day.

I watch YouTube over your shoulder,
a British comedian mocking her own

ignorance. Some days we watch old
sketches from our youth, our twenties,

thirties, forties. *Saturday Night Live* is the same age
as you are. We both mourned Chris Farley

and Phil Hartman before we knew each other.
Shared cultural markers that fade out,

come back into focus. Like emotions
that dip and rise. We are still here

before sunrise, laughing in the dark,
together, but each rolled in our own duvet.

My group message pings, a TikTok
from our favourite channel.

Separately we watch the video, share
our commentaries, react, remember,

yes, we are characters who have
each other.

NOTE

Previous versions of these poems have appeared in:
 Room
 Red Alder Review
 a fine. collection, vol. I (fine. press)

ACKNOWLEDGMENTS

Thanks and love to Daniel for being my #1 reader always, and reading this multiple times, and sharing a hotel room with my farts while taking me on the most perfect writer's retreat.

Thanks and love to nathan dueck for reading this manuscript when it was barely an idea and giving me just the right feedback and encouragement at the right time.

Thanks and love to Meghan Waitt for giving this the incredible combination of personal and literary feedback that I desperately needed and value so much.

Thanks and love to Jen Sookfong Lee for looking at this long poem and giving it her expert touch. I barely deserve her.

My editor ryan fitzpatrick is a true gem and this book would be nothing without him. He pushed me in the most wonderful way and engaged me in conversations I needed to have. He understood what I wanted to do and was an incredibly generous and fun editorial companion.

To everyone at Talonbooks, my poetry publisher ride or die, Catriona Strang, Charles Simard, Kevin Williams, Vicki Williams, Spencer Williams, Leslie Smith, Erin Kirsh, and Darren Atwater. I can't express how much I appreciate all you do.

And thanks and love to Jason for always supporting my work, especially this one where you feature so prominently.

DINA DEL BUCCHIA is the author of the short-story collection *Don't Tell Me What to Do* and of four other collections of poetry: *It's a Big Deal!*, *Coping with Emotions and Otters*, *Blind Items*, and *Rom Com*, the latter written with Daniel Zomparelli. She is the artistic director of the Real Vancouver Writers' Series and a co-host of the podcast *Can't Lit* with Jen Sookfong Lee. An otter and dress enthusiast, she lives on the unceded Territories of the xʷməθkʷəy̓əm, Sḵwx̱wú7mesh, and səlilwətał First Nations (Vancouver, British Columbia).

PHOTO: Chloe Krause.